Kids' Travel Guide
Paris

Flying Kids Presents:
Kids' Travel Guide
Paris

Writer: **Shira Halperin**

Editor: **Yael Ornan**

Designer: Keren **Amram**

Cover Designer: Francesca Guido

Illustrator: Liat Aluf

Translator: Oren Amir

Translation editor: Carma Graber

Published by FlyingKids

Visit us: www.theflyingkids.com

Contact us: leonardo@theflyingkids.com

ISBN: 978-1499677744

Acknowledgment: All images by FlyingKids except those mentioned below.

Shutterstock images: pp. 11, 12, 17, 19, 20, 22, 23, 24, 27, 34 & 35.

Table of Contents

Dear Parents,

If you bought this book, you're probably planning a family trip with your kids. You are spending a lot of time and money in the hopes that this family vacation will be pleasant and fun. Of course, you would be happy for your children to get to know the city to which you are traveling — a little of its geography, a little local history, important sites, culture, customs and more. And you hope they will always remember the trip as a very special experience.

The reality is often quite different. Parents find themselves frustrated as they struggle to convince their kids to join a tour or visit a landmark, while the kids just want to stay in and watch TV. Or the children are glued to their mobile devices instead of enjoying the new sights and scenery. Many parents are disappointed after they return home and discover that their **kids don't remember** much about the trip and the new things they learned.

That's exactly why the Kids' Travel Guides were created.

With the Kids' Travel Guides, young children become researchers and active participants in the trip. During the trip, kids will read relevant facts about the city you are visiting. The Kids' Travel Guides include puzzles, tasks to complete, useful tips, and other recommendations along the way. The kids will meet Leonardo — their tour guide. Leonardo encourages them to experiment, explore, and be more **involved in the family's activities** — as well as to learn new information and make memories throughout the trip. In addition, kids are encouraged to document and write about their experiences during the trip, so that when you return home, they will have a memoir that will be fun to look at and reread again and again.

The Kids' Travel Guides support children as they **get ready** for the trip, visit new places, learn new things, and finally, return **home.**

The *Kids' Travel Guide — Paris* focuses on the City of Light! In it, children will find background information on this special city. The *Kids' Travel Guide — Paris* focuses on 11 central sites that are recommended for children. At each of these sites, interesting blurbs, action items, and quizzes await your kids. You, the parents, are invited to participate or to find an available bench and relax while you enjoy your active children.

If you are traveling to Paris, you may also want to get the *Kids Travel Guide — France*, which focuses on **the country of France** — its geography, history, unique culture, traditions, and more. All with the fun and interesting style of the Kids' Travel Guide series.

Are you ready for a new experience?

HAVE A PLEASANT TRIP!

Hi, Kids!

If you are reading this book, it means you are lucky —
You are going to **Paris, France!**

You may have noticed that your parents are getting ready for the journey. They have bought travel guides, looked for information on the Internet, and printed pages of information. They are talking to friends and people who have already visited Paris in order to learn about it and know what to do, where to go, and when…

But this book is not just another guidebook for your parents.
This book is for you only — the young traveler.

So what is this book all about?

First and foremost, meet **Leonardo**, your very own personal guide on this trip. Leonardo has visited **many places** around the world (guess how he got there? 😊), and he will be with you throughout the book and the trip until you return home. Leonardo

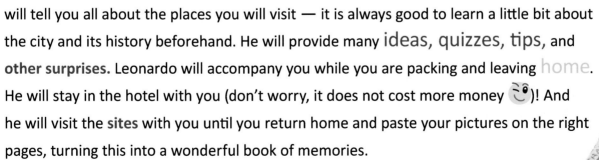

will tell you all about the places you will visit — it is always good to learn a little bit about the city and its history beforehand. He will provide many ideas, quizzes, tips, and **other surprises.** Leonardo will accompany you while you are packing and leaving home. He will stay in the hotel with you (don't worry, it does not cost more money 😉)! And he will visit the **sites** with you until you return home and paste your pictures on the right pages, turning this into a wonderful book of memories.

A Travel Diary –The Beginning!
Going to Paris!!!

How did you get to Paris?

By plane / train / car / other _____

Date of arrival _____ Time _____ Date of departure_____

All in all, we will stay in Paris for _____ days.

Is this your first visit _____ ?

Where will you sleep? hotel / campsite / apartment / with family / other _____

What sites are you planning on visiting?

_____
_____
_____

What special activities are you planning on doing?

_____
_____
_____

Are you excited about the trip?
This is an excitement indicator. Ask each family member how excited they are (from "not at all" up to "very, very much"), and mark it down on the indicator. Leonardo has also marked the level of his excitement…

not at all   very,
                                                   very much

Leonardo

Who is traveling?

Write down the names of family members traveling with you.

Name: ———————

Age: ———————

Has he or she visited Paris before?
yes / no

What is the most exciting thing about your upcoming trip?

————————————

————————————

————————————

Name: ———————

Age: ———————

Has he or she visited Paris before?
yes / no

What is the most exciting thing about your upcoming trip?

————————————

————————————

————————————

Name: ———————

Age: ———————

Has he or she visited Paris before?
yes / no

What is the most exciting thing about your upcoming trip?

————————————

————————————

————————————

Name: ———————

Age: ———————

Has he or she visited Paris before?
yes / no

What is the most exciting thing about your upcoming trip?

————————————

————————————

————————————

Name: ———————

Age: ———————

Has he or she visited Paris before?
yes / no

What is the most exciting thing about your upcoming trip?

————————————

————————————

————————————

Name: ———————

Age: ———————

Has he or she visited Paris before?
yes / no

What is the most exciting thing about your upcoming trip?

————————————

————————————

————————————

Paste a picture of the
whole family here.

Preparations at home — do not forget...!

Mom or Dad will take care of the packing of clothes (how many pairs of pants, which comb to take...). Leonardo will only suggest the stuff he thinks you should take with you when traveling to Paris.

As you are going on vacation away from home, Leonardo recommends that you take the following:

- *Kids' Travel Guide — Paris —* of course!
- comfortable walking shoes
- a raincoat (preferably folded, sometimes it rains without notice)
- a hat (and sunglasses, if you want)
- pens and pencils
- crayons and markers (It is always nice to color and paint.)
- a book
- your smart phone/tablet or camera

Tips!

Pack a few things for the flight in a small bag (or backpack), such as:

- snacks, fruit, candy, and chewing gum. It may help a lot during takeoff and landing, when there's pressure in your ears.
- games you can play while sitting down: electronic games, booklets of crossword puzzles, connect-the-numbers (or connect-the-dots,) etc.
- a notebook or a writing pad. You can use it for games, writing, or to draw or doodle in when you are bored...

Now let's see if you can find 12 items you should take on a trip in this word search puzzle:

P	A	T	I	E	N	C	E	A	W	F	G
E	L	R	T	S	G	Y	J	W	A	T	O
Q	E	Y	U	Y	K	Z	K	M	L	W	O
H	O	S	N	A	S	N	Y	S	K	G	D
A	N	R	Z	C	P	E	N	C	I	L	M
C	A	M	E	R	A	A	W	G	N	E	O
R	R	A	I	N	C	O	A	T	G	Q	O
Y	D	S	G	I	R	K	Z	K	S	H	D
S	O	A	C	O	A	E	T	K	H	A	T
F	R	U	I	T	Y	Q	O	V	O	D	A
B	O	O	K	F	O	H	Z	K	E	R	T
T	K	Z	K	A	N	S	I	E	S	Y	U
O	V	I	E	S	S	N	A	C	K	S	P

Leonardo, walking shoes, hat, raincoat, crayons, book, pencil, camera, snacks, fruit, patience, good mood

Welcome to PARIS

Paris, the capital of France, **is one of the most beautiful cities in the world,** if not the most beautiful of them all. If this is your first visit to Paris, you should know that it is situated on the **river Seine** and among its attractions are special streetlights, picture-like **gardens, impressive buildings,** famous cathedrals and museums, and excellent food!

Take a look around you: isn't it a beautiful city?

Did you know?
Paris is called "The City of Light."
Can you guess why?

Where did Paris get its name?

People lived in Paris as far back as 2,300 years ago (third century BC). About 1,500 years ago, it was named "Paris" by the King of the Franks, after the Parisii tribe who lived there at the time.

One of the most important people to leave his impact on Paris and the way it looks today was **Baron Haussmann,** who lived between 1809 and 1891. Paris was once **a small, crowded** town with no housing for the many people who settled there. Baron Haussmann started planning reforms: narrow streets became broad avenues, new buildings were built, and a system of underground railways was constructed. A system of sewers was dug and expansive gardens were laid out. Thanks to the Baron, Paris is such a beautiful city.

Did you know?
Paris is one of the most crowded cities in Europe. About 25,000 people live on each square kilometer (or less than half a square mile).

What does Paris look like?

Here is a map of the city.

If you take a close look, you can see that Paris is divided into sections and each section has a number. These sections are called **"arrondissements."** The center of the city is arrondissement number one.

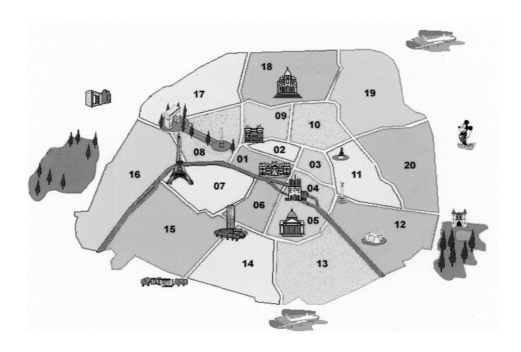

In which arrondissement are these monuments located?

Notre-Dame —————————————

Montasier Park —————————————

Arch of Triumph —————————————

Champs-Elysees —————————————

Eiffel Tower —————————————

The Louvre —————————————

Answers on page 38.

Things you see only in Paris

Paris is a very special city, and there are things you can find only there.

Take a good look around you: at the streets, the gardens, the buildings. Sniff the air, look at the stores.
Do you see some other things that make Paris special?
Write them down so you won't forget.

Wallace fountains

billboards

_____

_____

_____

_____

Did you notice the drinking fountains scattered throughout Paris?
These public drinking fountains are called **Wallace fountains** because they were a gift to the city from a rich Englishman named Sir Richard Wallace. He donated 50 fountains to the city 😮.

Transportation in Paris

There are several ways to get from one place to another in Paris. Here is some information, so you too will feel confident:

The first and fastest way is to use the **Metro.**
The French say that there is no place in Paris more than a five minutes' walk from a Metro station. This means you will not walk more than five minutes before you come across a Metro station, which will take you wherever you wish to go. This is very convenient.

Can you figure out what the main disadvantage of using the Metro is for tourists?

_____

_____

Did you know?
There are about 300 Metro stations in Paris.

This is the sign of the Paris **Metro** – whenever you see the letter "M" (it's not McDonald's...), you'll know there is a Metro station close by.

The second and more interesting way is by bus.
A bus can take you almost anywhere in Paris. The biggest advantage of traveling by bus is that you can see the city during the ride, meet other tourists, and take pictures as well (if the bus is slow and you are fast enough).

What do you think is the main disadvantage of traveling by bus?

_____

The third and most expensive way is by taxi.
The biggest advantage of traveling by taxi is being driven to your exact destination; there is no need to decipher a map or remember where to get off. If the driver happens to be nice, he will tell you about the places you pass by or at least answer your questions (for example, where is the best delicatessen in the area...), assuming you speak French, of course.

What do you think is the greatest disadvantage of traveling by taxi?

_____

The fourth, and most common way among tourists, is an open-bus tour.
Red double-decker buses travel all over Paris and pass by the city's famous historical places of interest. You can get off along the way, and later get back on. Travel by these buses is recommended for tourists who come to Paris for a short stay and want to see as many attractions as possible. Sit on the upper deck and you'll get a lovely view of the city from above.

What is the biggest disadvantage of taking a tourist bus?

_____

There is SO much to see in Paris — where to begin?

Museums, cathedrals, beautiful gardens, and of course, Disneyland Paris — there are plenty of attractions in Paris. You only have to choose! Now it's time for Leonardo to lend a hand — he has gathered information about the most recommended sites and activities.

Tip!
Plan the route of the tour with your family. Whichever way you choose, you can use a bookmark to find each site when you reach it.

In Paris:
Champs-Elysees

Ask anyone which is the most famous avenue in Paris, and the answer will always be — the Champs-Elysees! The Champs-Elysees is one of the central avenues in Paris, and one of its symbols known all over the world.

Champs-Elysees Avenue is **three kilometers (or almost one mile) long**. In its upper part, there are gardens and palaces, among them the lovely Elysees Palace. In the lower part, there are prestigious **shops** and office buildings.

Tip! The oldest puppet show theater in Paris is located on the Champs-Elysees. It was founded about 200 years ago and is called Guignol (pronounced Gee-nyawl). It is highly recommended that you buy tickets to one of the shows. It is a wonderful experience!

A map of the street –

When you take a walk along the avenue, mark the places you see on this map (beautiful stores you like, impressive buildings, and such).

Concorde Square

Disney Store

Arch of Triumph

The Champs-Elysees

My impressions of the Champs-Elysees:

Which is the most beautiful store?

_____

Which is the largest store?

_____

Did we buy anything? If so, what?

_____

L'Arc de Triomphe (the Arch of Triumph)

The Arc de Triomphe is a monument built by Napoleon in honor of his army, to commemorate the victory in the Battle of Austerlitz (where Napoleon's army beat the Russian and Austrian armies). The building of the Arch lasted 30 years, and unfortunately, Napoleon did not make it to the inauguration parade.

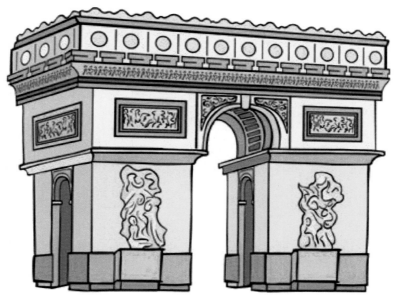

Did you know?
In order to finance the building of the Arc de Triomphe, Napoleon imposed a tax on the French citizens, making them donate 10 percent of their income 😟 .

The names of soldiers and officers killed in battle, and the names of the major battles of the Napoleonic Wars, are inscribed on the walls of the monument. The battles he lost are not mentioned on the Arch... 🙂

It doesn't matter from which direction you approach the Arch, the closer you get, the bigger and more **impressive it looks**. When you stand underneath, it appears

enormous!

Climb to the upper part of the Arch. It is 45 meters (or almost 148 feet) high, and the view from the top is marvelous.

Did you know?

The building of the Arch took a long time and when Napoleon's troops entered Paris, only the laying of the foundation was completed. A creative solution was found: a mock-up of the Arch, made of wood and cloth, was erected and decorated for the victory parade.

The Arc de Triomphe stands in the center of the Place Charles de Gaulle (read about him later on), formerly named Place de l'Etoile, which means "star" in French. There are 12 avenues diverging from the square (in memory of Napoleon's 12 victorious battles), reminding one of a **star**.

Arc de Triomphe

Help Leonardo to find the street names. Write each name in order, in its proper place.

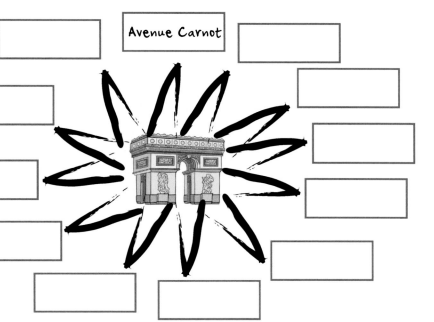

Avenue Carnot

Answers on page 38.

19

The Eiffel Tower

The Eiffel Tower is one of the most famous towers in the world. In 1887, the French were looking for a **structure** to mark the centennial (100 years) celebration of the French Revolution. One hundred architects and engineers sent their proposals, detailing how the structure should look.

Gustave Eiffel was an engineer who specialized in the planning and building of enormous bridges, which were unusual back then. He suggested erecting a huge metal tower. The Eiffel Tower opened to the public exactly **100 years after the French Revolution**. About five million people visit the Tower each year.

Eiffel Tower

Quizzes!

How tall is the Eiffel Tower?

a. 5 meters (16-1/3 feet)
b. 30 meters (98-1/2 feet)
c. 324 meters (1,063 feet)
d. 1 kilometer (3,281 feet)

 Tip!

If you are interested in the history of the Tower and would like to know how it is painted and kept clean, watch the film that is screened on the first level of the Tower.

Answer: C - 324 meters (1,063 feet)

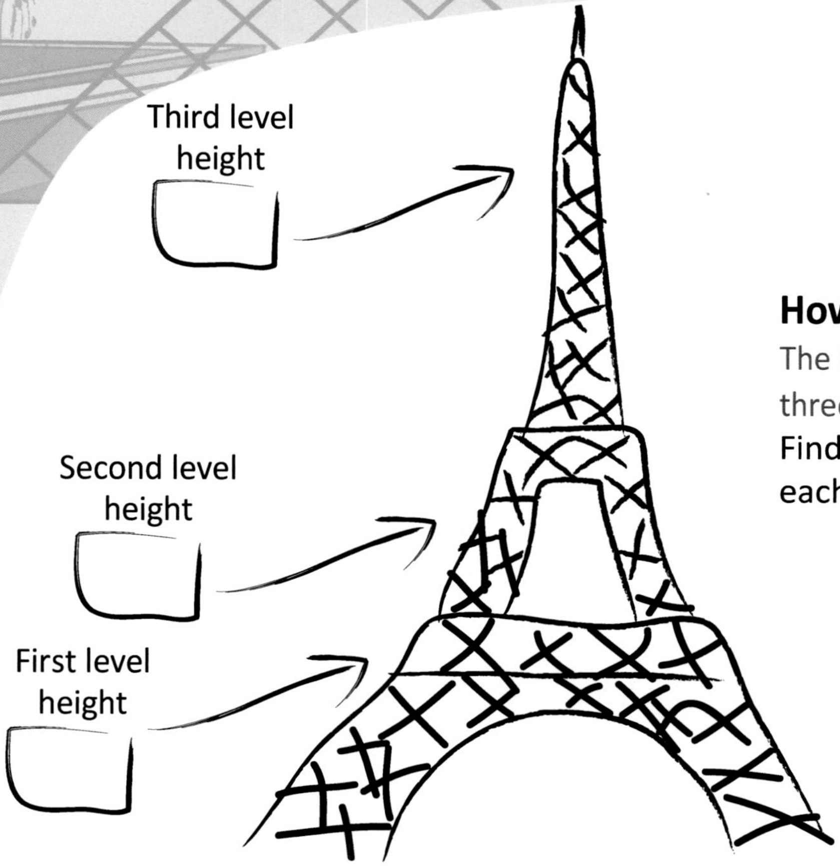

Third level
height

Second level
height

First level
height

How is the Tower built?

The Eiffel Tower is divided into three main levels.
Find out where the height of each level is written.

When you reach the first level, choose a spot from which to take a picture.

Which spot did you choose? _____

Can you find the same spot on each level and photograph it from different heights?

Answers:
1. 57 meters (187 feet)
2. 115 meters (377-1/4 feet)
3. 276 meters (905-1/2 feet)

To reach the top of the Tower, you must climb 1,652 stairs .
Even if you are willing to face the challenge, it is impossible:
tourists can climb the stairs up to the second level
only, and from there upwards, there's an elevator .

A few things not everyone knows about the Eiffel Tower:

- The height of the Tower changes between summer and winter by 15 centimeters (about 6 inches). The metals it is made of shrink and expand according to the weather: when it is cold, the metal shrinks — and when hot, it expands.

- When a strong wind blows, the Tower swings from side to side, 12 centimeters (4-3/4 inches) in each direction.

- They used 2.5 million rivets to build the Tower.

- Up **until 1930**, it was the **tallest structure** in the world.

- Five hundred people are employed in the Tower: 250 in maintenance, and 250 in the restaurants, the police station, and the post office.

- About 16,000 people visit the Tower every day!

Did you know?
About 100 years ago, the Tower was going to be dismantled. But there was a need for a tall structure to be used as an antenna for communication purposes, and luckily, it was allowed to remain. It's hard to imagine Paris without the Eiffel Tower!

Centre Pompidou (the Pompidou Center)

The Pompidou Center is actually a **huge museum** of modern art.*
But there is still a lot to see and do in the Centre Pompidou, even if you don't visit the museum itself to see paintings and works of art.

Should we go there?

Yes! For several reasons: First and foremost, the building itself is completely different from any building you've seen so far in Paris. **It looks as if it were built by children from Lego blocks and colorful pipes.**
Street performers, jugglers, and mime artists perform in the plaza in front of the museum. It's **fun** to sit on one of the benches or wander among the performances. It's a free show! Another reason to go is the escalator. It's true that most kids have gone up and down escalators, but have you ever used an escalator outside a building?

*If you are interested in finding out more about abstract art and what can be found in museums, you can buy our special *Kids' Travel Guide — Paris Museums.*

What is inside the building?

We will let you discover this by yourselves...

A hint: much more than works of art!

When you enter the building and walk around, write down what you see. (We will help you a little...)

We've already said that this building is different from what you've seen so far. When Georges Pompidou, who was the President of France at the beginning of the 1970s, decided to construct an art center (bearing his name, of course 😉), a design competition was held and more than 600 architects presented some very strange plans.

It seems that Pompidou was a very daring president, given that this is the plan he chose... 😃 At first, many French people were angry when they saw the building, and some even ridiculed it.

What do YOU think of the building?

amazing ☐

funny ☐

ridiculous ☐

beautiful ☐

unique ☐

ugly ☐

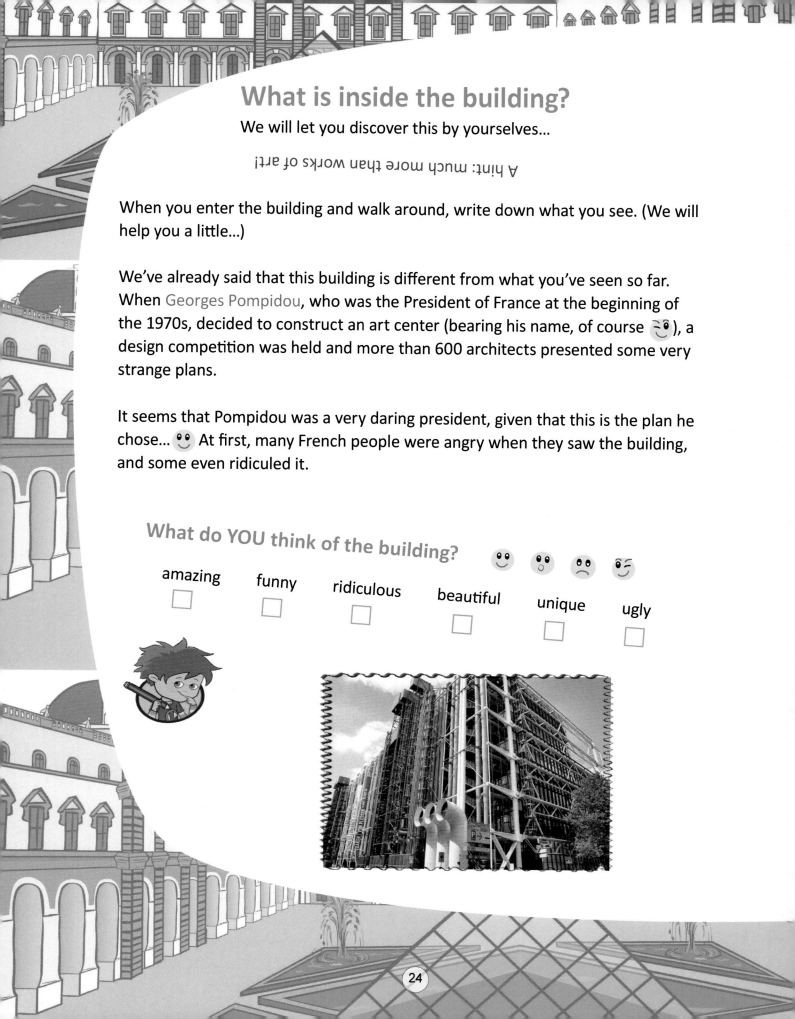

The architects who planned the Center decided that instead of hiding the electric, water, and air-conditioning systems, they would emphasize them and use them as decoration. Each color represents a different system:

The blue pipes are the air- conditioning system.
The green pipes are the water system.
The yellow pipes are for electricity.
The red pipes indicate the location of the stairs and elevators.
The white pipes are the ventilation pipes of the underground tunnels.

What other artists did you see or activities did you do? Write them here.

Stravinsky Square

Have you ever seen so many pretty, different-looking fountains?
Although this square is named after the famous composer **Igor Stravinsky**, these beautiful fountains were made by the sculptors **Jean Tinguely** and his wife, **Niki de Saint Phalle.**

Here you can see the pool at the Stravinsky Square without the fountains....
Write the number of each fountain in the right space in the pool.

2

15

4

6

5

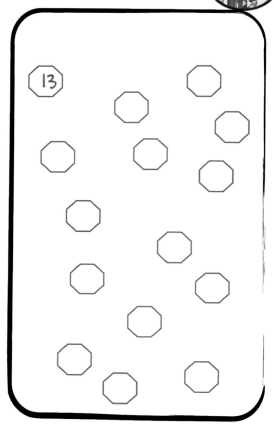

13

Can you figure out which fountain is missing? Draw it here.

8

1

9

11

7

13

3

10

14

Answers on page 38.

26

Notre-Dame Cathedral

Notre-Dame Cathedral is one of the most famous churches in Europe. It took 167 years to build the cathedral 👀. During the building, kings and rulers came and went, and each one **introduced changes** according to his tastes and to the style of the time.

The original cathedral was built of **wood**, and was completed in 1345, more than 662 years ago. Since then the building has been **remodeled** so many times that almost none of the original parts remain.

The South Tower –
Here are the famous bells from which Quasimodo swung in the book and movie *The Hunchback of Notre-Dame.*

The Rosette –
This was built more than 700 years ago. On either side of the circle are statues of Adam and Eve.

Kings Gallery –
The 28 statutes of kings of Israel and Judah are displayed here.

Three Gates –
They present themes from the world of Christianity. The central gate is dedicated to Jesus. The right gate shows Christian figures, and the left has Jewish figures.

Try to guess the diameter of the Rosette (the big circle in the middle).

Answer: 9 meters (29-1/2 feet)

Tip! How can Leonardo recommend you visit the cathedral without mentioning the book *The Hunchback of Notre-Dame*? The book was written by the famous French author **Victor Hugo,** and it tells about Quasimodo, the deaf hunchback who rings the bells of the cathedral and falls in love with Esmerelda, the beautiful gypsy. The book became more famous when Walt Disney Studios turned it into a wonderful movie. Leonardo strongly recommends that you read the book when you return home, or at least watch the movie. (It is possible, of course, to read the book **and** to see the movie 😊).

Did you know?

A few things that not everyone knows about Notre-Dame Cathedral.

- During World War I the French were afraid that the bombing would damage the cathedral and destroy the **ancient windows**. They therefore removed all the windows and stored them in a safe place. When the war ended all the windows were returned to their places.
- There is a giant pipe organ in the cathedral containing 7,800 pipes (900 are original). In 1992 a special program was initiated to **computerize the organ** and to connect it to the local communications network. The position of organist at Notre-Dame is considered to be one of the most desirable jobs in France.
- Until the Eiffel Tower was built, the Cathedral was the **highest spot** in Paris.

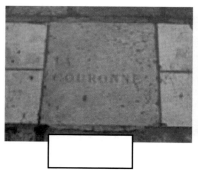

Tiles with the names of streets and sites in Paris inscribed on them are embedded along the square in front of Notre-Dame. Find the tiles in the pictures. Mark each of the pictures above with a ✔ when you find the tile in the square.

La Defense

From far away you can see that the **La Defense** area is unique in Paris. The whole area is built of glass and concrete and looks a little like it doesn't belong to the local scenery.

The meaning of La Defense is "The Defense." Just like the Arch of Triumph, it was built in honor of the French army. (Do you remember which leader built the Arch of Triumph? That's right — Napoleon!) La Defense was also built as a huge arch, this time in modern style. The arch was built in honor of fraternity, which means "brotherhood," and is one of the three symbols of the French Revolution: **FREEDOM, EQUALITY, FRATERNITY**. The arch was dedicated at a special ceremony, marking the 200-year anniversary of the French Revolution.

The arch is 35 stories high and you can take an elevator to the roof.

Go up on the roof and look southeast (you can easily spot the direction if you look for a long boulevard full of cars). What do you see from up there? Check off the sites that you see with a checkmark, and the sites you don't see with an X.

- [ ] The Seine River
- [ ] The Louvre
- [ ] Charles de Gaulle Airport
- [ ] Champs-Elysees
- [ ] EuroDisney
- [ ] Tuileries Gardens
- [ ] Parc de Villette
- [ ] The Picasso Museum
- [ ] The Arch of Triumph
- [ ] Notre-Dame Cathedral
- [ ] Concorde Square

IMMIGRATION OFFICER
* (4034) *
10 MAY 1999

And now write the names of the sites, from the closest (#1) to the farthest (#5).

1 _____

2 _____

3 _____

4 _____

5 _____

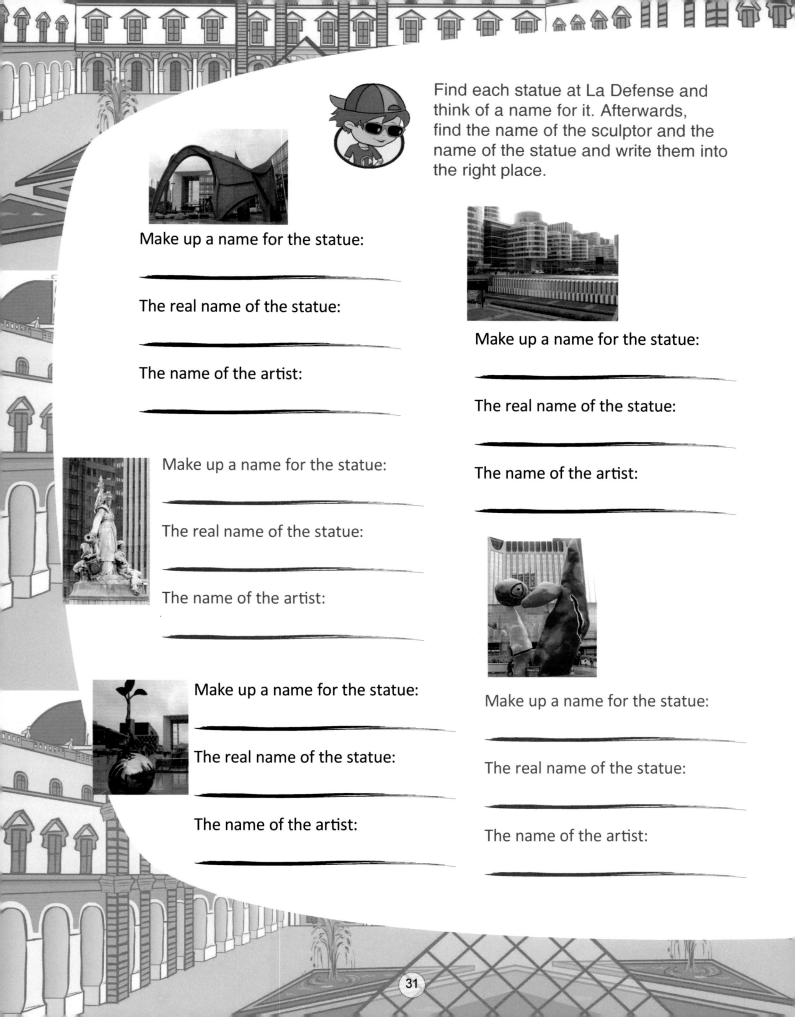

Find each statue at La Defense and think of a name for it. Afterwards, find the name of the sculptor and the name of the statue and write them into the right place.

Make up a name for the statue:

The real name of the statue:

The name of the artist:

Make up a name for the statue:

The real name of the statue:

The name of the artist:

Make up a name for the statue:

The real name of the statue:

The name of the artist:

Make up a name for the statue:

The real name of the statue:

The name of the artist:

Make up a name for the statue:

The real name of the statue:

The name of the artist:

Tuileries Gardens

Welcome to the prettiest park in Paris.

In the past the park was closed to the common people, and only the royalty were allowed to visit. Luckily for us, now it is open to everyone, **and anyone who wants** can visit and enjoy a little nature in the middle of Paris.

Did you know?

Tuileries means "shingles." There are those who say that this is because there used to be a shingle factory in the park, and there are others who say that it is because of the special roof, made of **shingles**, on a palace that stood where the park is today. The palace burned down, and today there is a gallery called "Jeu de Paume" in its place.

Help Leonardo get from one end of the park to the other.

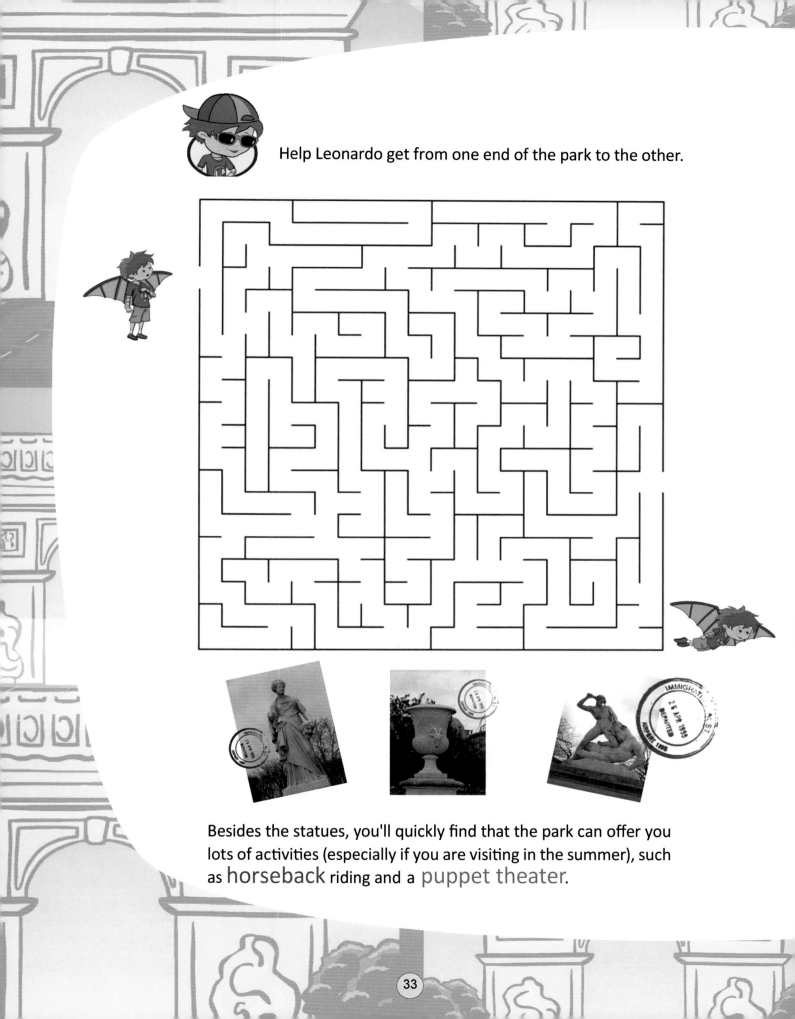

Besides the statues, you'll quickly find that the park can offer you lots of activities (especially if you are visiting in the summer), such as horseback riding and a puppet theater.

Triumphal Arch of Carousel

Does this arch look familiar? If so, you can probably guess who ordered it made.

That's right, it was Napoleon!

Stand **in front** of the arch and look around you. What do you see?

_____

What do you think of the Triumphal Arch of Carousel?

_____

Concorde Square

Concorde Square is one of the most famous squares in Paris. It took more than 10 years to build. At first it was called Louis the 15th Square, but since then it changed its name and we'll tell you why:

This square has a **terrible story,** and there is not one French citizen who hasn't heard it. In his will, King Louis the 15th ordered that a square be built in his name. And so a square was built with a **fancy statue** of the king in the middle 😞.

obelisk

Thirty years later the French Revolution broke out, and its leader decided to execute all the opponents of the revolution, using a guillotine. They changed the name to "Revolution Square," took down the statue of the king, and in its place, put up a **guillotine.*** So it happened that the son of King **Louis the 15th** (called, of course, Louis the 16th), and his wife, Queen Marie Antoinette, were executed in this square. And they weren't alone: more than a thousand protesters were put to death in this square.

***What is a guillotine?** It is a device that was used for cutting off the heads of people who opposed the revolution.

The symbol of Concorde Square is the obelisk.

What is an obelisk? A type of monument that is tall and skinny with a point at the top.

The **obelisk** in Concorde Square is a present given to King Louis Philippe in 1829 from Muhammed Ali, the ruler of **Egypt.**

Yes, it is a very big and heavy gift 😊 : it is 23 meters (75-1/2 feet) high and weighs 250 tons.

Did you know?
The real tip of the obelisk was stolen many years ago and never made it to France. The obelisk was capped with a golden tip instead.

And what about the symbols that are inscribed on the obelisk?

These drawings are called hieroglyphics — the writing system that the ancient Egyptians used. Although the obelisk was a present to the French, the hieroglyphics describe an Egyptian victory by King Ramses II. On the bottom, you'll find a description and drawings of how they managed to bring this giant thing from Egypt to France.

What is found around the obelisk?

_____

_____

Write down the appropriate number next to each part:
1 is the highest and 7 the lowest.

Can you remember the names of the sites that appear in the illustrations?

(A hint: You can use a map.)

 1

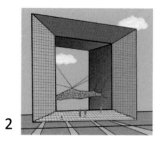 2

 3

 4

 5

 6

Answers: (1) Triumphal Arch of Carousel; (2) La Defense; (3) Arch of Triumph; (4) Tuileries Gardens; (5) The Louvre Museum; (6) Concorde Square

Answers

Paris

Monuments (page 11)

Notre-Dame	4th arrondissement
Montasier Park	14th arrondissement
Arch of Triumph	Between the 16th and 17th arrondissements
Champs-Elysees	8th arrondissement
Eiffel Tower	Between the 7th and 15th arrondissements
The Louvre	1st arrondissement

The Arch of Triumph (page 19)

The names of the streets in Place Charles de Gaulle (de l'Etoile) in order:
1. Avenue Victor Hugo
2. Avenue Kleber
3. Avenue d'iena
4. Avenue Marceau
5. Avenue des Champs-Elysees
6. Avenue de Friedland
7. Avenue Hoche
8. Avenue de Wagram
9. Avenue Mac Mahon
10. Avenue Carnot
11. Avenue de La Grande Armee
12. Avenue Foch

Stravinsky Square (page 26)

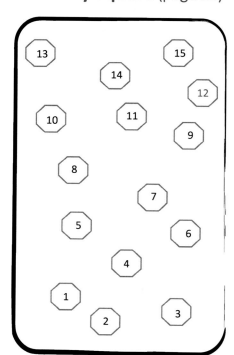

And to sum it all up...

Summary of the trip

We had great fun, what a pity it is over...

How long did we stay in Paris?

_____

At which hotel did we stay?

_____

What kinds of transportation did we use?

_____

Which sites did we visit?

_____ _____

Our most favorite place in Paris is: _____

The souvenirs we bought in Paris are: _____

The best food we ate in Paris was: _____

Grade the most beautiful places and the best experiences of your journey:

> **First place –**

> **Second place –**

> **Third place –**

A journal

Which places did
we visit?

What did we do?